Wings at War Series, No. 2

Sunday Punch in Normandy

THE TACTICAL USE OF HEAVY BOMBARDMENT
IN THE NORMANDY INVASION

An Interim Report

Published by Headquarters, Army Air Forces
Washington, D. C.

Office of Assistant Chief of Air Staff, Intelligence
From Reports Prepared by Eighth Air Force

New Imprint by the
Center for Air Force History
Washington, D. C. 1992

Wings at War

COMMEMORATIVE EDITION

Originally published shortly after key air campaigns, the Wings at War series captures the spirit and tone of America's World War II experience. Eyewitness accounts of Army Air Forces' aviators and details from the official histories enliven the story behind each of six important AAF operations. In cooperation with the Office of the Secretary of Defense, the Center for Air Force History has reprinted the entire series to honor the airmen who fought so valiantly fifty years ago.

Washington, D.C.

Foreword

Sunday Punch in Normandy focuses on the all-important invasion of Normandy, on June 6, 1944, forever remembered as "D-Day." Just before dawn, wave after wave of Army Air Forces heavy bombers targeted the beach areas to make way for the assault troops. The pilots encountered virtually no air opposition, because the massive Allied air superiority effort had been brilliantly planned and well-orchestrated.

This short study describes in detail the close cooperation among the Allies in formulating the D-Day plan. A final section on operations gives a chronology of the interdiction missions flown by Eighth Air Force fighters and bombers.

CONTENTS

ILLUSTRATIONS

OFFICIAL PHOTO USAAF

Lt. Gen. Carl Spaatz, Commanding General, United States Strategic Air Forces

The Tactical Use of Heavy Bombardment in the Normandy Invasion

Planning The Operation

ENGLAND was bulging with troops. Along the narrow lanes dispatch riders dashed. Tanks lumbered over the roads; assault craft were piled at distribution points; frequent and elaborate exercises were being staged. Already there had been practice alerts, when all personnel were required to be at their bases. Newspapers speculated, the German press and radio exulted that the Allies had missed the most favorable tides and could not assault for another month. Tension ran high.

For months there had been good-natured badgering between members of the Eighth and Ninth Air Forces, who in turn had banded together when assailed by ground force personnel. Now they were beginning to realize that they were all members of a bigger team, an outfit which would soon be called upon to conduct history's greatest military operation.

Forgotten now were differences between strategic and tactical, between ground and air, between Army and Navy, between Americans and their Allies. All were welded into one compact, devastating fist, set to deliver the Sunday punch.

There are more facets to the Normandy invasion than to a finely cut diamond. Volumes and sets of volumes will be written about it. This booklet considers only one, the tactical employment of the Eighth Air Force heavy bombers before and during the invasion and the resultant change in the disposition and use of Eighth Air Force fighters.

It required careful planning. Here are shown the planning steps, with the problems which arose and demanded workable solution. Also included is a summary of Eighth Air Force operations from D minus 4 to D plus 11.

Like the other participating components, the Eighth Air Force, commanded by Lt. Gen. James H. Doolittle, did its part in highly creditable fashion.

* * *

The plan for invasion envisaged air operations on a comprehensive and unprecedented scale. These were divided into two phases. The aim of the first was the attainment of Allied air supremacy and destruction of the enemy's productive capacity to the point where, once the projected foothold on the Continent had been secured, overwhelming matériel superiority could be brought to bear. The second phase had as its objective effective air cooperation with the ground assault.

A vital share in the preparatory operations was allotted to the strategic bomber forces of the Royal Air Force and the U. S. Eighth Air Force. In the second phase the Ninth Air Force and the Second Tactical Air Force (RAF) were in the forefront, but again the strategic forces made important contributions.

On 15 April 1944 the over-all air plan for the employment of all British-based aircraft in cooperation with the forthcoming invasion of France was formally issued by Headquarters, Allied Expeditionary Air Force, having been originally drafted some 6 weeks earlier. It contained detailed provisions for operations and furnished the basis for extensive preparations by the Eighth Air Force to fulfill its considerable proportion of the over-all assignments. A directive from Lt. Gen. Carl Spaatz's headquarters, USSTAF, dated 30 May 1944, confirmed earlier informal directions requiring the rendition by the Eighth Air Force of maximum cooperation according to provisions of the air plan and related documents.

Between 15 April and 6 June practically everybody had a hand in formulating the plan, which changed so often and so much its final form was only a distant relative of the original. The commanders of all the principal air, ground, and naval forces in the theater worked on it. Details were suggested, developed, polished by committees of staff representatives and technical experts. When formally published, it represented the knowledge and opinions of men who knew their jobs. A brief chronology of the more important planning phases can be traced as follows:

1. The AEAF was created on 15 November 1943, with Air Chief Marshal Sir Trafford Leigh-Mallory designated as Air Commander in Chief. Headquarters, AEAF, was thereafter represented at the 21st Army Group meetings, and the basic requirements of air cooperation were established, subject to the general policies already formulated by the Combined Chiefs of Staff.

2. A Joint Planning Committee was formed on 15 December 1943 by Headquarters, 21st Army Group, to consider the relationship of air power to the assault plan, the delay of enemy reserves, coordination with naval fire, and neutralization of coastal artillery. When Headquarters, AEAF, became fully organized and staffed, an Operations Plans Section was constituted, which gradually took over the functions of the Joint Planning Committee.

3. Of more immediate significance to the Eighth Air Force was the formation on 10 January 1944 of the AEAF Bombing Committee to plan specifically the employment of bomber aircraft. Principal considerations were:

a. Suitability of targets for bombing
b. Relationship of bombing commitments to the scale of effort estimated to be available
c. Allocation of priorities to the various commitments
d. Apportionment of the available bomber effort

Supplementing the AEAF Bombing Committee almost from the start was the Operational Planning Committee, consisting of certain members of the first-named body plus representatives of the 21st Army Group and each of the air forces involved. The work of the two committees was so closely interrelated that no separate assessment of their contributions toward the final detailed plans is possible. The function of both was to transform into concise and exact operational programs the general policies agreed upon by the air, ground, and naval commanders. Designated to represent the Eighth Air Force on the Operational Planning Committee was a senior operations controller, but as the earlier meetings concerned primarily the commitments of the tactical air forces, his attendance was required only occasionally until 15 April 1944. Before and during this period, specific problems pertaining to heavy-bomber operations were often submitted by letter to USSTAF or Eighth Air Force for solution.

By 25 May, details of the Eighth Air Force program were largely completed. On 29 May, Air Chief Marshal Leigh-Mallory requested each headquarters concerned to appoint a regular member of the committee, prepared to meet daily. Thereafter until 30 June, the Eighth Air Force representative was in constant attendance day and night.

To facilitate complete understanding between the Eighth Air Force and the principal Army headquarters, SHAEF granted permission for direct contact between USSTAF and Eighth Air Force representatives, on the one hand, and American and British Army staff officers, on the other. Two such meetings were arranged, at which very important concrete agreements were reached. The first involved the commander and staff of the American First Army Artillery, and the second was with staff officers of the I and XXX Army Corps of the British Second Army. Final coordination of air activities was achieved through informal meetings among representatives of the various commands.

Daily meetings of air force commanders were begun on D minus 3 and continued throughout the critical period of the invasion. Final alterations in plans were considered and decided upon, as well as the transitory problems arising as the invasion forces moved inland after the initial foothold had been secured.

Eighth Air Force Aims and Commitments

Heavy Bombers

Before considering the tactical program involved, it is well to summarize briefly the strategic role previously enacted by the Eighth Air Force, together with RAF Bomber Command. This role, designed to provide indirectly for the ultimate success of the invasion, was incorporated in the Combined Bomber Offensive Program, its aim having been defined as "the progressive destruction and dislocation of the German military, industrial, and economic system and the undermining of the morale of the German people to a point where their capacity for armed resistance is fatally weakened."

Pertaining more directly to the success of the invasion was the corollary development of a specific bombing program against the German aircraft industry. This program was directed at the attainment of virtual air supremacy and as such was indispensable to operations by ground forces. It was not until the summer of 1943 that

TACTICAL TARGET. A good concentration of bombs on the Angoulême marshalling yard, scored by Eighth Air Force heavy bombers.

631804—45——2

the Eighth Air Force could operate in sufficient strength to execute sustained large-scale attacks, but its efforts in those summer months were sufficient to keep the GAF from creating enough front-line strength to stop subsequent major operations. Adverse weather during November and December prevented the cumulative bombing necessary for complete success in such an undertaking, but production levels had been affected to the extent that the Luftwaffe had done little more than maintain its strength during 1943.

A more intensive campaign was possible during the early months of 1944, reaching a peak of sustained effort during the period 20–25 February and maintained, subject to tactical considerations, until the end of May. The substantial damage to factories and assembly plants, coupled with destruction in aerial battle of German first-line combat aircraft by both bombers and escorting fighters on a hitherto unprecedented scale, was unquestionably the decisive factor in reducing the GAF to the point where it had no more than a nuisance value during the critical invasion period. This was attested by the remarkably low number of sorties directed against the Allied beachheads and shipping lanes.

The following figures give some appreciation of the war of attrition by the Eighth Air Force against the GAF. During the first 6 months of 1944, 6,813 bombers dropped 16,522 tons on aircraft factories, and 8,257 bombers dropped 21,267.7 tons on airfields and air parks. In the same period 1,914 first-line enemy aircraft were destroyed by the bombers in aerial combat and 1,682 were destroyed or damaged on the ground as a result of bombing of air parks, airfields, and factories. To these figures can be added the impressive total accounted for by escorting fighters—1,696 destroyed in combat and 761 in strafing attacks. Results obtained against other strategic targets were not so strikingly apparent in relation to D-day operations, but evident shortages in fuel, tanks, motor vehicles, radar equipment, and ammunition were traceable, at least in part, to the strategic bombing of the Eighth Air Force and the RAF Bomber Command.

During April and May 1944 continuation of attacks against strategic objectives was necessary to prevent reconstruction and as a means of holding the greater part of the GAF within Germany. At the same time the first commitments directly associated with the impending assault came into force. (There were also attacks against installations near the French coast when the weight of Eighth Air Force bombing was required in addition to the continual operations by tactical air forces.) These initial commitments consisted of attacks against 20 marshalling yards in occupied territory and neutralization of all active GAF operational bases within a 350-mile range of the invasion beaches.

To avoid giving any clue as to the probable assault area, attacks on both target categories were widespread, the marshalling yards being key points throughout the rail network of western Germany, Belgium, and northern and eastern France, and the airfield targets including the more important bases in northern Germany. The purpose of the Transportation Plan was primarily the destruction of repair and maintenance facilities and only incidentally the tearing up of trackage and damage to locomotives and rolling stock. By these means it was hoped to prevent the enemy from effecting rapid concentration of men and matériel, cut the flow of supplies and reinforcements from Germany, and force increasing reliance upon road transport, thus promoting wastage of fuel and motor vehicles and offering targets most suitable for fighters and fighter-bombers. Pursuant to this plan, 3,469 bombers dropped 9,520 tons on marshalling yards in Germany, France, and the Low Countries during the month of May. These attacks were so successful that the Eighth Air Force was able to bomb additional targets not assigned in the original list.

The Airfield Plan was designed to deprive the Luftwaffe of bases within effective striking range of the assault beaches by destruction of permanent installations for repair, maintenance, and servicing, and by cratering runways and landing grounds to an extent that fields would be unusable. Parked aircraft destroyed in these attacks would constitute a further blow against the enemy's dwindling front-line strength. It did not prove feasible to conduct operations against all such targets, but the most important were hit and a good percentage was effectively neutralized. From D minus 30 and D minus 21, respectively, the scope of the attacks against rail and airfield targets was considerably narrowed, but special care was taken in the selection of targets so as not to reveal the actual invasion area. Airfields attacked were confined to those within a 130-mile radius of Caen and in the Brest-Nantes region, to compel German fighters to operate from bases at least as far distant from the beachhead as those of the Allied tactical forces.

In addition, it was agreed with the Naval Chief of Staff that the Eighth Air Force would undertake to attack bases for submarines and light naval vessels if diversion of effort from other commitments was feasible. Only one such attack was undertaken, and adverse weather prevented its successful completion.

Throughout this preliminary period, wherein the original commitment against strategic objectives was modified by the Transportation and Airfield plans as well as by the occasional attacks required against coastal installations, the Eighth Air Force, nominally under the control of SHAEF from 14 April 1944, was allowed to retain freedom of decision in fulfilling its varied assignments. This greatly facilitated operations, as priorities could be carefully balanced against weather factors and other operational considerations by those best qualified to cope with the problems of heavy-bomber operations. Not until 1 June 1944 did control under the fixed schedule provided for in the over-all air plan for the invasion pass to Headquarters, AEAF.

Immediately prior to D-day (D minus 3 through D minus 1) Eighth Air Force operations were to be twofold in nature, consisting of final attacks against rail junctions and airfields as well as missions against coastal installations. The postponement of D-day brought into effect a previously prepared schedule of targets in the same categories. Their size and the identification problems which they presented made the probability of direct hits very small, and, even if hit, the concrete emplacements were of such thickness that little harm was likely to result. During this short period prior to D-day, bomber forces were to be carefully husbanded to nsure that the necessary strength for the comprehensive D-day program was maintained. Therefore, the operations for each day were to employ only 50 percent of the available strength with one important exception: if visual conditions prevailed over Germany on either D minus 3 or D minus 2, 100 percent of the effort was to be expended, 40 percent against the usual tactical targets and 60 percent against strategic objectives within Germany. The latter mission was designed as a final attempt to contain enemy fighter strength for defense of Germany until the last moment before the actual landings.

The most important and by far the most elaborate D-day plans concerned the first mission of the day, involving attacks immediately prior to H-hour against 45 coastal installations between the Orne and the Vire estuaries on the Normandy coast of France. The 6 mile coastal strip included all assault beaches except an adjacent American beach, designated as Utah, which was the responsibility of the U. S. Ninth Air Force.

Some 1,200 heavy bombers were to participate, flying in squadrons of six aircraft. Following a carefully devised system of predawn assembly aided by searchlights, navigation lights, Aldis lamps, buncher and splasher beacons, and Gee equipment, the aircraft were to fly predesignated courses to the target area, bombing in successive waves until H-hour (or thereafter attacking secondary targets well inland). Assault craft were to remain 1,000 yards offshore until H-hour, and a 5-minute interval was to elapse between the releases by the last wave of bombers and the initial touchdown by the assault troops. These safety factors represented the final compromise between the desire of the ground forces to exploit immediately the demoralization resulting from the bombing at the risk of casualties and the inclination of the air forces to impose considerably greater intervals to minimize the dangers from possible bombing errors.

Demoralization of enemy front-line defenders and disruption of communication lines for reserve forces were the sole aims of the pre-assault bombing. It was understood that only a small percentage of the actual targets would suffer direct hits and smaller still would be the number seriously affected. Bomb loadings were established of 100-lb. GP, 120-lb. fragmentation, 500-lb. GP, and 1,000-lb. GP, the last for installations well clear of the beaches. Fuzing was to be instantaneous to avoid cratering the beaches except for targets away from the landing areas, where 1/10 nose-1/100 tail was permissible.

Alternative plans were provided for bombing through overcast, since it had been agreed that, other factors being favorable, the ground assault would be initiated whether or not visual bombing was possible and, if necessary, entirely without bomber cooperation, in which event the Eighth Air Force was to be in constant readiness. Minimum requirements for visual attacks by heavy bombers were an 8,000-foot ceiling, 3-mile visibility, and sufficient breaks in any low cloud to permit ready target identification. Less favorable conditions would demand the substitution of the plan involving overcast technique. Pinpointing of targets would be impossible, but since demoralization and immobilization of enemy forces were the principal aim, it was considered that area bombing of the sectors wherein lay the specific visual targets would provide virtually the same effect.

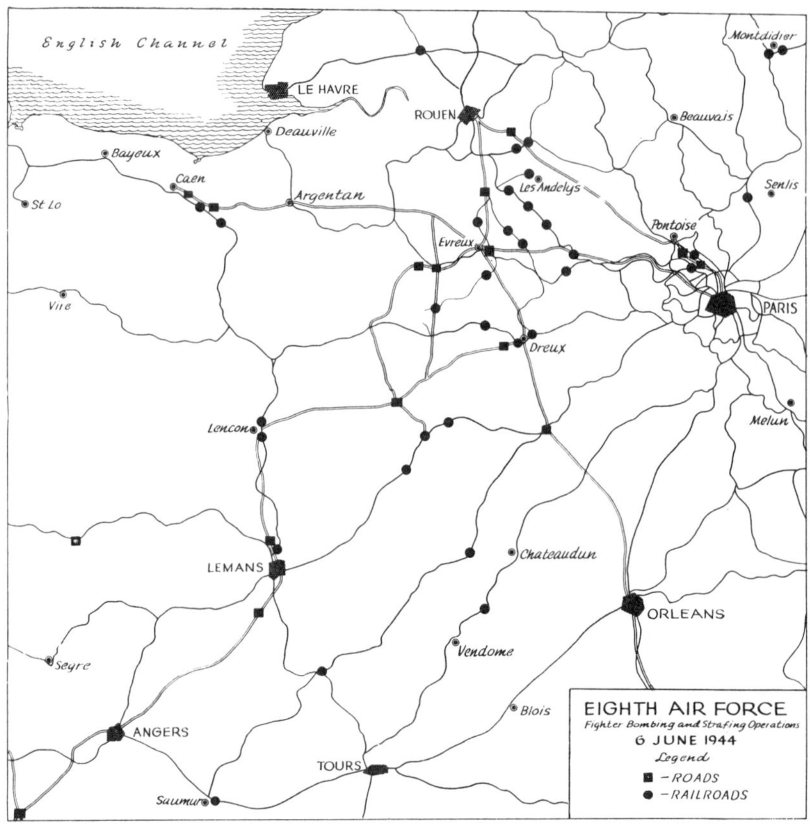

Squadrons were to fly six abreast and bomb on the release of a Pathfinder aircraft in one of the center squadrons. By such an arrangement deflection errors were largely neutralized, but further safeguards against errors in range were deemed necessary. Accordingly, the interval between the final bombing and the initial touchdown was to be increased to 10 minutes. One other necessary change was the instantaneous fuzing of all bombs, since the entire attack was to be directed against the assault beaches, which must not be cratered. Since the Ninth Air Force aircraft were not equipped for overcast bombing, provision was needed to cover Utah beach in their stead, should it prove impossible for even the medium bombers to operate beneath the cloud base.

Subsequent to the assault phase, additional missions were laid on in cooperation with the landing operations. Targets outlined in the over-all air plan consisted mainly of transportation choke-points, including several Normandy towns through which ran important lines of communication. Leaflet warnings were to be dropped to the populace of these towns before bombing.

Weather, photographic, and visual reconnaissance missions, special supply operations to the French Forces of the Interior, leaflet-dropping sorties, and radio countermeasure flights were to be undertaken in conjunction with the over-all ground and air activities.

No exact schedule of operations subsequent to D-day could be prepared in advance, since the progress of the ground forces and the nature of the enemy's reaction would be the determinants, but certain general features of the program were decided upon. Detailed target material, covering virtually all known potential tactical objectives in northern France, received the required distribution well in advance of D-day. Attacks were to be continued against road and rail transport facilities, including bridges on the Brest peninsula and across the Loire River; enemy airfields; concentrations of enemy reinforcements and supplies; and coastal defenses in the Pas de Calais sector. Blasting of robot-bomb launching sites was also contemplated if the security of the British Isles called for such action.

Requests for specific attacks were to be forwarded from Headquarters, AEAF, when the Eighth Air Force representative was in regular attendance. It was anticipated that a number of these missions would have to be undertaken on very short notice. The interval prior to a return to strategic bombing was dependent upon the degree of success attained by the ground forces, and it was recognized that even after the need of continual cooperation by heavy bombers had passed there would be periodic demands for tactical operations.

Fighters

No marked deviation from the normal escort tasks of Eighth Air Force fighters was required until D-day. Early in 1944, following substantial increases in fighter strength, the policy had been inaugurated of executing strafing attacks upon completion of escort duties. Such attacks became an accepted adjunct to high-altitude escort and, due to the tremendous scale of activity, provided the best possible training for ground-cooperation missions. On days when no heavy-bomber operations were scheduled, it was often possible to dispatch the fighters on independent bombing and strafing missions, some in the nature of experimental attacks against airfields and bridges. To a large degree, experience gleaned from these missions equipped fighter pilots for the job ahead.

The first fighter commitment to become effective on D-day was the protection of Allied shipping during daylight hours. P–38's were detailed to this task because of their readily identifiable lines and also because this fighter, relatively less effective than the P–47 and the P–51 at high altitudes, can operate without handicap at 3,000/5,000 feet, the altitude designated for these patrols. The four P–38 groups operating under the direction of the Combined Control Center at Uxbridge and in conjunction with Ninth Air Force P–38 groups were to work under the Type 16 ground control station at Ventnor; thereafter, Fighter Direction Tender No. 13 would be stationed in mid-Channel and would assume control. Each of four sectors was to be covered by one P–38 squadron, flying in 90-minute patrols according to a predetermined schedule.

On D-day the other Eighth Air Force fighters, four P–47 and seven P–51 groups, were to support all American and British bombers operating during daylight hours in the vicinity of the assault area by means of continuous area patrols east, south, and west of the beachhead, patrols which would also serve to form a protective screen around the ground forces. The cover area was bounded approximately by the Seine on the east and the Loire on the south and, to avoid identification difficulties, excluded the actual assault locality where Ninth Air Force and Second Tactical Air Force fighters would be operating.

These operations were to be conducted in accordance with three well-formulated plans, two for the two peak periods of bomber effort, dawn and late afternoon, and one for the intervening period of less activity. To avoid continuous patrols the fighter groups were divided into two units, an "A" group of two squadrons to fly during the peak hours and a "B" group of one squadron for the in-between period.

An important secondary function, subordinate to bomber support, was the execution of strafing and bombing attacks at the end of area patrols or on independently scheduled missions when the bombers were not operating. It was expected that more emphasis would be given to this type of operation subsequent to D-day. The principal aim of such activities was the destruction of enemy road and rail transport and the interdiction of all types of enemy movement toward the assault area. Target priorities were established as follows:

1. Enemy rail transportation
2. Enemy road transportation
3. Ammunition dumps
4. Troop concentrations
5. Airfields

Although direct control of the P–38's was to pass to the tactical fighter forces' Combined Control Center, the operational and executive control of the Eighth Air Force groups was to remain the responsibility of Eighth Air Force and VIII Fighter Command, which also had the task of preparing the detailed plans for implementing the over-all assignments.

Transition From a Strategic to a Tactical Role

Heavy-bomber operations in close cooperation with ground forces involved a tactical concept differing greatly from familiar strategic bombing activities. Problems were posed in relation to assemblies, formations, routings, bomb loadings, fuzings, and overcast bombing techniques; details of briefing and mission reporting had to be worked out; coordination with other air forces and with naval planners was necessary to a far greater degree than heretofore required; aircraft recognition and delineation of prohibited bombing zones had to be considered. Most important, the requirements of the ground forces must be translated into a workable air cooperation program, and the ground force commanders had to be thoroughly informed as to the capabilities and the limitations of the heavy bombers. Differences arose and were generally compromised, although a few were submitted to SHAEF for final settlement. The over-all plan was of such paramount importance that practice exercises were necessary to settle many points, often on a large scale and sometimes integrated with the execution of operational flights. Rehearsals of certain features of the program were undertaken to assure successful performance at the critical time. The more important problems, and the steps taken to solve them, were:

Predawn assembly

The initial D-day bomber program called for take-off and assembly during hours of darkness on an unprecedented scale. It was believed that the use of radio aids, flares, and navigation lights would permit

631804—45——3

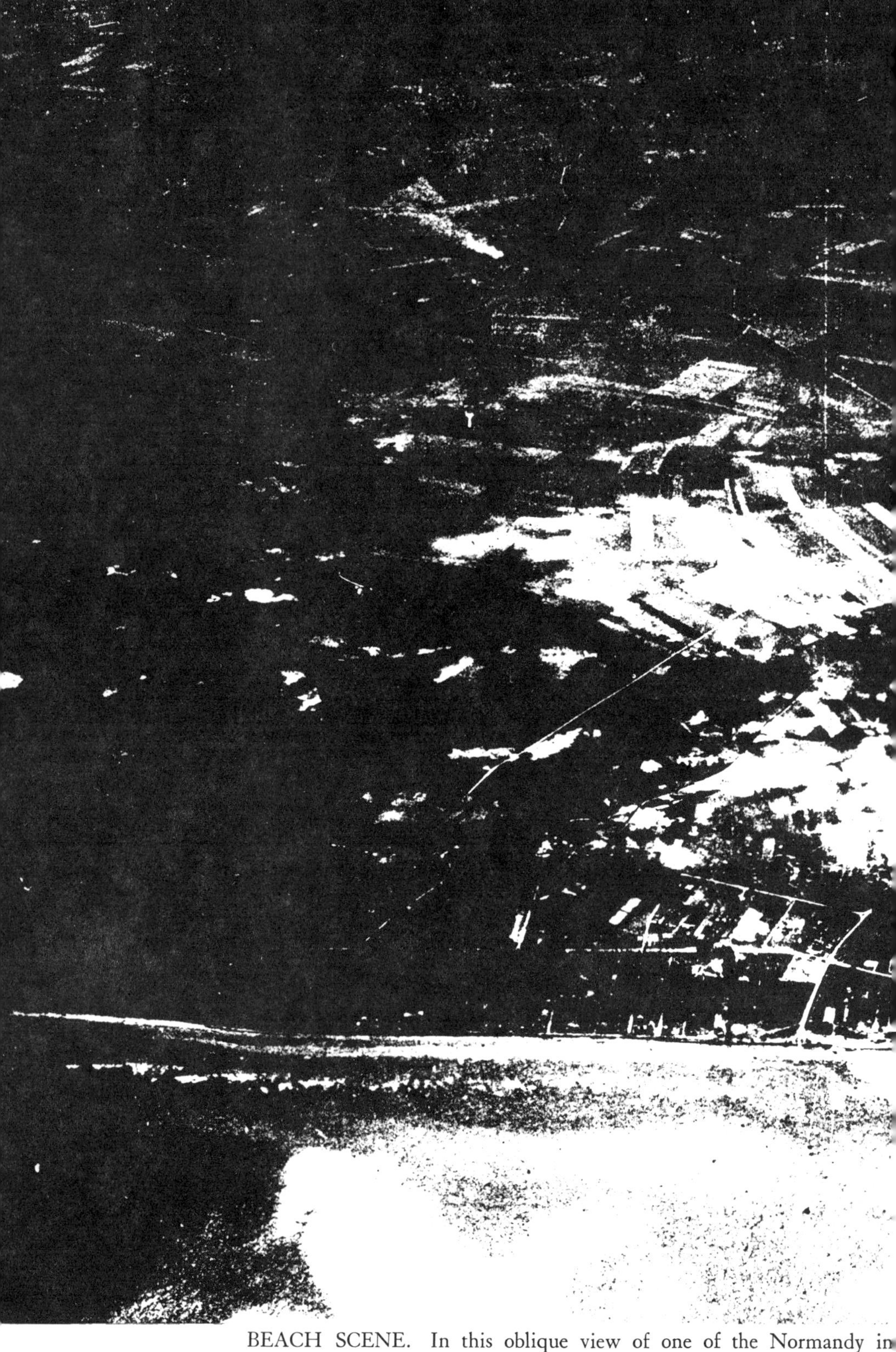

BEACH SCENE. In this oblique view of one of the Normandy in
spread before th

ıches it is possible to see the blast damage resultant from the bomb carpet
g ground forces.

successful accomplishment, but it was deemed wise to have a trial operation. This was conducted on 1 May before a regular bombing mission. It involved nine groups of 21 aircraft each from each of the three bombardment divisions, with aircraft assembling in specified areas during the hours of darkness and following designated routes to the south coast and back to the base areas. The aircraft in each group were dispatched in three waves, the first composed of nine-plane squadrons and the second and third of six-plane squadrons. The exercise was completely satisfactory, and on the basis of this test the six-plane squadron was adopted for the D-day missions.

Routings

While the usual consideration of route planning prevailed, the necessity of assuring recognition of aircraft by naval vessels employed on convoy operations resulted in placing restrictions on flights over the shipping lanes. One of these forbade any aircraft except fighters on shipping patrol to fly over the convoy areas from the direction of the combat zones or the Pas de Calais. Because of this, and in connection with the use of Pathfinder equipment, it was decided to prescribe a course for the initial D-day mission directly from the south coast of England to the Normandy beaches and returning south and west of the Channel Isles.

Loadings and fuzings

Extensive research was conducted to determine the types of bombs and fuzings to be used. An AEAF Weapons Committee, with four representatives of the Eighth Air Force, was established to consider these questions, and several practice bombing missions were conducted, the most comprehensive being held on 26 April, in which 12 nine-plane flights were sent to the Studland Bay bombing range to determine the effect of 100-, 250-, and 500-lb. bombs with various fuzings. It was learned that fragmentation and 100-lb. HE bombs would be most effective against personnel, vehicles, wire entanglements, and gun positions not emplaced. Recommendations based on these findings were incorporated in the over-all air plan.

Overcast bombing technique

The possibility of having to use Pathfinder instruments for initial D-day bombing missions was considered, and the relative merits of both H2X and GH were weighed. On the basis of operational experience and tests the former was selected. This decision resulted from the lower average range error to be expected from H2X as compared with GH when the former was operating against targets located in such a manner that water and land appeared simultaneously on the scope at right angles to the line of approach, the definition in such instances being particularly clear. This factor was an important consideration in the selection of the north-south approach. Deflection errors did not constitute hazards on this axis of attack. The limited number of GH aircraft available was a further consideration, since accuracy would be seriously impaired if a very large number of units was releasing on relatively few Pathfinders, and the possibility of equipment failures on these few Pathfinders would have a proportionately large effect on results.

Visibility trials

Accurate determination of earliest and latest times practicable for visual bombing was of vital import to the exact establishment of H-hour. A visibility trial was conducted by aircraft of the Eighth Air Force, the Ninth Air Force, and the 2d Tactical Air Force, operating against simulated targets in England (an infantry platoon, field artillery battery, coastal battery, small village, roads in open and wooded areas, railway lines, and coastal and inland towns). Results of this operation were forwarded to Headquarters, AEAF, on 24 May 1944 for use in the determination of H-hour.

Briefing and interrogation

The security aspect was a primary consideration of the briefing, and it was decided that efficiency would not be impaired if air crews were not given the essential information prior to the normal pre-mission briefing. Exception was made in the case of Pathfinder navigators and bombardiers, who were specially briefed some days in advance. At the briefing, stress was laid on the importance of avoiding premature bomb releases because of the tremendous Allied assemblage offshore. Normal time limits for interrogation and submitting mission reports were revised in the interest of expediting the flow of information regarding results and observations. A system of tactical reporting was accordingly set up whereby preliminary reports were to reach Eighth Air Force Headquarters within 45 minutes after first landings and detailed intelligence reports within 2 hours. A comprehensive staff coordination trial was held involving the issuance of specimen field orders, briefing for three simulated D-day missions, fictitious take-off and landing times, and flash and intelligence reports.

Aircraft recognition and demarcation of friendly lines

The dangers inherent in the inability of Allied units—air, sea, and ground—to ascertain without delay the hostile or friendly character of combat aircraft were recognized and precautionary steps were taken. Prohibited zones for certain types of aircraft were established, principally over the shipping lanes and assault area, thus allowing naval and ground forces unrestricted freedom to fire at aircraft other than stated types or approaching from other than certain directions.

Another measure was the institution of distinctive markings for aircraft. Except the four-engine bombers, all planes were painted with wide alternate black and white stripes on wings and fuselage. The converse problem of defining areas for combat aircraft in order to avoid bombing and strafing within friendly lines was largely overcome by the adoption of a bomb line. Beyond this line (one predetermined for the 6 hours immediately after H-hour, another for the remainder of D-day, and thereafter subject to daily changes as decided by air and ground staffs) ground forces ventured at their peril and targets could be attacked at will. Behind this line no bombing or strafing was to be conducted without specific arrangement with the ground forces, and the originator of such a request was to assume the responsibility for clearing the region around the targets chosen for attack.

Ground force requirements

Certain adjustments in the bombing desired by Army planners were necessary to conform to bomber capabilities. When requests for destruction of fixed defenses, explosion of mine fields, cutting of underground cables, elimination of barbed-wire entanglements or antitank obstacles, demoralization of front-line troops, delay and disruption of reserve elements, and the blocking of transport by bombing French towns—when such requests were submitted by Army commanders it was necessary to point out the probable degree of success against each type of objective and then to secure priority ratings so that the bomber strength could be apportioned as desired by the ground forces.

In many instances the destructive effect necessary could be obtained only by use of heavy bombs with delayed fuzings, which would cause the cratering the Army wished to avoid. The probability was emphasized that direct hits on gun emplacements would not be in excess of 2 percent of the tonnage dropped and that in most instances little damage would result. Nevertheless, the Army requested that the attempt be made to destroy those on the flanks of the beaches, believing that some emplaced positions could be put out of action, at least temporarily, and that craters in this area would afford valuable protection to assault troops sent to capture these strong points. Otherwise it was agreed that the air cooperation should aim primarily at the demoralization of front-line troops, with a possible bonus in the destruction of barbed wire and other hazards. No request was made for the elimination of underwater mines or obstacles. The Army commanders were informed of the possibility of gross errors causing casualties among troops in assault craft and accepted them as a necessary risk.

Selection of targets

Certain categories of requested targets were not deemed by Eighth Air Force to be satisfactory for heavy-bomber attack. In three instances the matter was submitted to SHAEF for determination. The first concerned marshalling yards in occupied territory, and objection was based on the belief that medium bombers would be adequate, that the damage could be readily repaired and hence would not justify the effort expended, and that the proximity to built-up areas would result in civilian casualties and property damage outweighing the disruption of enemy communications. The second case involved the bombing of bridges. It was considered that the nature of these targets would require a very great expenditure of effort in relation to probable damage achieved and the erection of temporary spans could largely nullify successes gained. In the third instance the matter concerned choke-points in French towns which the 21st Army Group desired to have blocked by rubble in order to delay enemy reinforcements. The stand of the Eighth Air Force was based on the risks to civilian lives and property. In all three cases SHAEF, motivated by military expediency, directed that the attacks be made. Arrangements were made to drop warning leaflets sufficiently in advance of the last-mentioned type of attack to enable the civilians to evacuate the threatened areas.

Over-all Air Cooperation Plan

In order to envisage the scope of the Eighth Air Force role in the projected over-all air effort, the commitments, as previously enumerated, may be compared with the following aims of the entire aerial program:

1. To attain and maintain an air situation whereby the German Air Force is rendered incapable of effective interference with Allied operation
2. To provide continuous reconnaissance of the enemy's dispositions and movements
3. To disrupt enemy communications and channels of supply by air attack
4. To support the landing and subsequent advance of the Allied Armies
5. To deliver offensive strikes against enemy naval forces
6. To provide air lift for airborne forces

Delivering The Punch

SUCH careful planning as has been related in some detail in this narrative merited gratifying results. In the following section the operations of the Eighth Air Force from 2 June through 17 June are examined.

D-day was the day for which so many thousands of ground-force troops had been eagerly waiting. This was their day to take over, which they did in magnificent fashion, adding new luster to proud regimental and divisional names. How the Eighth Air Force teamed with them is shown in the succeeding pages.

Operations 2–17 June 1944

THIS discussion is divided into two sections, one dealing with bombers and the other with fighters. The bomber assignment, separated into three time periods, was carried out as follows:

D minus 4 to D minus 1 (2–5 June)

Within this period the job of the Eighth Air Force was to continue attacks against transportation and airfield targets in northern France, and to institute a series of blows against coastal defenses, a majority situated along the Pas de Calais coast. A final effort to contain German fighters within the Reich as late as possible by conducting a deep penetration against strategic targets had been planned for this period, but adverse weather interfered.

This phase of the program was performed according to plan. A total of 3,386 bombers participated in the eight missions flown and 9,387.45 tons were dropped for the loss of 14 bombers.

Substantial damage was inflicted upon airfield and rail transport targets. Few of the coastal defenses were seriously affected in proportion to the effort put forth, but this had been anticipated, the more so since Pathfinder technique was necessary in most instances. Since deception as to the actual landing area was the primary purpose of the attacks against this latter type of target, the operations may be regarded as successful, for, as far as can be ascertained, the landings along the Normandy coast had the advantage of complete tactical surprise.

D-day (6 June)

The first mission was concerned primarily with neutralization of coastal defenses and demoralization of German front-line troops immediately prior to the landings. The other three missions were

OFFICIAL PHOTO USAAF

Lt. Gen. James H. Doolittle, Commanding General, Eighth Air Force

directed at the severance of communication lines between the beachhead defenders and reserve elements, with targets consisting largely of road choke-points in Caen and several smaller Normandy towns.

The first, third, and fourth missions were accomplished substantially as planned, employing overcast technique exclusively in the first and third and for several targets in the final mission. The second mission was not generally prepared for bombing through the overcast, and clouds over the targets prevented attacks except in the case of one formation which bombed a secondary target on the indications of the only Pathfinder aircraft participating. A total of 2,698 bombers participated in the day's operations and 3,596 tons were dropped for the loss of three bombers.

Assessment of damage caused during this day's operations was rendered difficult by the fact that a majority of the targets attacked were cloud-obscured and strike photographs were therefore unrevealing. In many instances follow-up operations were executed before reconnaissance cover was obtained. The beachheads were subjected to fire from naval guns, rockets, and mortars, and were bombed by aircraft of other commands, with the result that a definitive evaluation of damage was not possible. Information from surveys conducted by air force representatives, interviews with ground personnel, and prisoner-of-war interrogations may be summarized in the following manner:

1. The immediate beach areas showed only limited evidence of bomb damage, as was to be expected in view of the extra precautionary measures taken to avoid short bombfalls when through-the-overcast bombing technique was used. These precautions included the arbitrary time delays on bomb releases. Areas behind the beachhead, ranging from 300/400 yards to 3 miles, revealed extensive evidence of concentrated bombing patterns.
2. The principal contribution made by this bombing effort was the demoralization of enemy troops and the disruption of signal and transport communications, which hindered the deployment of immediate reserves.

In regard to the limited number of targets where damage was assessable from strike or reconnaissance photographs, results varied with cloud conditions encountered.

The noteworthy feature of D-day cooperation by heavy bombers was the fact that the beaches were bombed by airplanes flying above a solid overcast of clouds. While a carpet of bombs placed in front of the advancing troops was deemed highly desirable, the danger to our own soldiers from bombs dropped without visibility of the ground demanded most careful consideration.

Had it been necessary to make the decision several months earlier, it is likely that such a project would have been abandoned. By the use of through-the-overcast technique, Eighth Air Force bombers had been known to miss targets by wide margins. However, in preparation for D-day, against the possibility that weather would prevent visual bombing, especially selected navigators and bombardiers had been diligently trained in H2X technique, and repeated tests had been conducted against shore-line targets. These tests showed that accuracy was possible, and that the greatest menace to the safety of friendly troops was the danger of inadvertent and premature bomb releases. This risk was carefully weighed by the ground commanders against the advantage of a bomb carpet to clear their assault path. Confronted with photographic evidence of the accuracy of bombing tests, they elected to take the risk. This decision was a resounding vote of confidence in H2X equipment and in Eighth Air Force crews.

Briefing was precise, pointed, and personal. All watches must be exactly synchronized; careful attention must be given to all mechanical details; the bombing must be far enough in front of the ground forces to minimize any chance of hitting them, yet near enough to give the bomb carpet its maximum effectiveness. "Here are your friends and brothers," the airmen were told. "You won't see them, but they're there, depending on you. Don't hit them, but get your bombs on that shore line!"

If the decision to bomb ahead of our troops through overcast was breath-taking in its boldness, the results were epochal. A short distance offshore lay the LST's and other craft carrying the invading force. Confident of cooperation from planes they could not see, the men of the assault wave started ashore at the precise instant established beforehand. Exactly on schedule the first wave of bombers came over, laying its bombs on the shore line and proceeding inland. The entire force of bombers had to clear the attack point within 5 minutes or run the risk of dropping bombs on friendly forces. Absolutely according to plan the heavy bombers performed their mission, laying their carpet of bombs before the attacking Allies. So effective was their bombing, and with such a minimum of damage to friendly forces was the operation carried out, that many lives were saved. Ground commanders were lavish with their praise. Another milestone of modern warfare had been passed.

D plus 1 to D plus 11 (7–17 June)

Attacks aimed at the interdiction of enemy road and rail transport, with special emphasis laid on bridges over the Loire and the rivers of Brest peninsula; the denial to the German Air Force of the use of airfields and landing grounds within effective range of the beachhead; and the destruction of supply sites in northern France—these were the principal tasks allotted to the Eighth Air Force during the 11 days immediately following D-day. Toward the end of this period, a resumption of strategic bombing was contemplated, but unfavorable operating conditions over Germany resulted in prolonging tactical operations, although two missions against oil refineries in Germany were possible, at Emmerich on 14 June and Misburg on 15 June.

Scheduled assignments were carried out by the great majority of units involved in the operations during this period, although through-the-overcast bombing technique was frequently necessary. Participating in the 13 missions executed were 9,801 bombers; bombs dropped totaled 20,365.6 tons; losses were 41 aircraft.

Considerable success was achieved toward restriction of enemy movements by attacks on road and rail junctions, marshalling yards, choke-points and bridges. Notable was the destruction or severe damage caused to at least 16 road and rail bridges across the Loire River and rivers on the Brest peninsula. Operational airfields and landing strips in northern France were also successfully bombed, and many were rendered completely unserviceable by the destruction of permanent installations and the postholing of runways and landing grounds. Due principally to the necessity for employment of overcast technique, little damage was accomplished in the operations against the supply sites.

Fighters

Air cooperation

The first consideration in planning daily fighter operations during the period 2 to 17 June was adequate escort of all heavy-bomber missions of the Eighth Air Force. (On D-day the escorted forces included various other Allied air units.) The interdiction commitment, bombing and strafing of tactical targets on the perimeter of the battle region, could be undertaken only after the requirements for cover of bombers had been fulfilled. In fact, the limited enemy air reaction for the period as a whole made it possible to detail squadrons from supporting groups to execute attacks against ground installations even before the completion of their primary task, thus supplementing the bombing and strafing operations of groups which had not been needed for support.

In the majority of instances the bomber targets were closely located and the penetration involved was so shallow that ample escort was provided by assigning groups to patrols in areas in which the objectives were located or through which the bombers passed en route to and from them. On a few occasions the location of objectives made it necessary to assign all available groups to close escort, and in other instances a combination of area-type patrol and close escort was employed.

Claims against enemy aircraft resulting from aerial combat were 148 destroyed, 6 probably destroyed, and 58 damaged. Thirty friendly fighters are known to have been lost in engagements with the enemy.

Interdiction

The VIII Fighter Command's work during the period 6 to 17 June, that of preventing or delaying enemy movements with bombing and strafing attacks on lines of communication, was highly effective. These operations were carried out in areas on the perimeter of the assault zone, fighter operations over the battle area proper being the responsibility of the Ninth Air Force and 2d TAF.

Because little enemy air opposition was expected on 6 and 7 June, it was possible for fighter-bombers to operate on these days in small units of one and two squadrons. This plan enabled the harassing attacks to be more continuously maintained and allowed the Command to operate over a wider area than would have been possible had full groups been employed. As the enemy increased his fighter strength in France, this plan had to be abandoned because small units would have been subject to possible heavy losses. In this connection, full groups were employed on fighter-bomber missions on and after 8 June with either one squadron in each group as top cover for two fighter-bomber squadrons or one group covering one or two other groups executing such attacks.

From 6 to 17 June, a total of 335 fighter-bomber attacks, in all instances by units of 8 aircraft or more, were made against tactical targets, 147 against railway marshalling yards, sidings, junctions, and tracks, 87 against bridges, 38 against mobile rail transportation, 26 against road transportation, and 37 against various other targets. During this period 1,339.3 tons of bombs were dropped.

The over-all results achieved by bombing and strafing operations are not reflected by a mere examination of claims for the period, which are by no means complete. In many instances there was not sufficient time between sorties for detailed interrogation, while in others the participating groups described results in general terms, i. e., excellent, good, etc., without submitting specific claims. The following claims against rail and road transportation are believed to represent the minimum results obtained against such targets:

Target	*Destroyed*	*Damaged*
Locomotives	118	70
Railroad cars	375	1,258
Trucks	607	533
Tanks	16	31
Armored vehicles	12	15
Staff cars	7	10
Other vehicles	80	36

These claims afford a graphic indication of the scale of the fighter effort toward isolation of the beachhead area, but a further and very significant contribution was made by the ever-present threat of attack against rail and road transport which seriously impeded enemy movements by day.

Shipping patrol

From 5 to 10 June the four P–38 groups of the Command were committed to the execution of shipping patrols under the direction of the Combined Control Center. On 11 June, three groups and, from 12 to 15 June, two groups were used for this purpose. During these 11 days a total of 2,887 sorties were flown. None of the fighters was lost, but five sustained Category "E" (salvage) damage. Throughout the entire period, no enemy aircraft was encountered over the shipping corridor by groups of the VIII Fighter Command.

During the period 2 to 17 June, 15,773 fighters of the VIII Fighter

Command were dispatched on operational missions and 15,086 sorties were flown for the loss of 155 aircraft. Of these losses, 48 were attributed to antiaircraft fire, 30 to enemy aircraft, and 25 to accident. Causes of the losses in 52 instances are unknown. Total claims against enemy aircraft were 201 destroyed, 6 probably destroyed, and 82 damaged, of which number 148 destroyed, 6 probably destroyed, and 58 damaged resulted from aerial combat and 53 destroyed and 24 damaged from attacks on enemy airfields.

Subsidiary Operations

In addition to the major operational roles executed by Eighth Air Force bombers and fighters, other units performed important complementary functions. These consisted of weather and photographic reconnaissance missions, leaflet-dropping operations, radar-jamming flights, and special supply drops to the French Forces of the Interior. There were 501 sorties flown and seven losses in the course of these operations, which directly or indirectly contributed to the success of the over-all undertaking.

Enemy Air Reaction

Calculations that enemy air opposition to the initial landings would not be on a heavy scale were borne out by the Luftwaffe's behavior. Our ground forces were both surprised and gratified at their relative freedom from air attacks.

It is of interest to examine just what the GAF was doing for several days before the invasion started, and then during the assault phase:

Dawn 28 May–Dawn 4 June

During the night of 28–29 May some 70 enemy aircraft, consisting of Ju–88's, Ju–188's, Me–410's, and FW–190's, operated against Britain. There was an armed reconnaissance of the Sussex coast by 10 FW–190's and Me–410's, and 50 Ju–88's and Ju–188's carried out minelaying operations between Teignmouth and Start Point. There were 10 Me–410's on intruder patrols over East Anglia. Bombs fell on Worthing, Hove, Lyme Regis, Torquay, and Paignton areas.

An armed reconnaissance of the eastern Channel was carried out by some 90 Ju–88's, Ju–188's and Me–410's on the night of 29–30 May, and minelaying and a bombing attack took place in the Falmouth

TACTICAL TARGET. Le Mans Airfield, hit by Eighth Air Force heavy bombers in conjunction with the Normandy assault.

area early on 30 May. *Despite very favorable weather during the early part of the week, the absence of known overland reconnaissance aircraft west of Portsmouth was most noticeable. In view of the increasing imminence of Allied landing operations, this lack of interest in covering south coast regions as a whole was remarkable.*

Strong fighter reaction was provoked by major Allied raids on central and eastern Germany and Poland. The main effort was made on the 28th, when about 450 single-engine and 50 twin-engine fighter sorties were flown, of which approximately 200 were encountered near Dessau and the remainder in the Magdeburg and Strasbourg localities. It is estimated that 300/350 sorties were flown on 29 and 30 May. The reactions to attacks on France, Belgium, and western Germany remained negligible. Only slight reaction was aroused by RAF Bomber Command night missions to targets in France and Belgium.

Bombs fell at Falmouth and scattered points between Hampshire and Sussex on 1 June. Possible intruder operations on the night of 31 May–1 June were carried out by about 15 ME–410's, six of which were overland and dropped bombs in the Norwich region.

FW–200's from Trondheim carried out long-range reconnaissance on 5 days of the week, and Ju–290's from southwest France on one day. Other reconnaissance activity was generally on a low scale. Of two Ju–88 reconnaissance aircraft observed in the Orkneys-Shetlands area on the 30th, one was destroyed east of Kirkwall and the other came overland at Lerwick. Two Me–109 reconnaissance aircraft were destroyed south of the Isle of Wight on the 29th.

Dawn 4 June–Dawn 11 June

If more evidence is needed that the Allied landings in Normandy achieved complete tactical surprise, consider that there was no appreciable air opposition until the night of 6–7 June, when some 175 long-range bomber sorties are estimated to have been flown against shipping off the Cherbourg coast and against targets on the beachheads, including 55 sorties by aircraft carrying torpedoes and radio-controlled bombs. All available types of aircraft were used, including torpedo-carrying units from the south of France, but the attacks, especially those on shipping, appear to have been a complete failure.

Similar operations, including minelaying, were carried out on the following night, although the scale of effort fell off to about 160 sorties and to 100 or fewer on succeeding nights, probably because of bad weather.

Both long-range bomber and torpedo-bomber operations were conspicuously ineffective. The scale of effort was possibly below that anticipated due to unexpected weakness of the long-range bomber force; there had been no evidence of long-range bomber activity by daylight.

Small intruder operations were carried out off and over East Anglia on the night of 7–8 and 10–11, with an estimated 10 aircraft participating in each. Day and night reconnaissance was flown over the beachheads and the Channel, with fairly regular cover of the Straits and the Thames estuary as far as the Suffolk coast, and over the southern part of the North Sea.

For at least four nights of that week, Ju–290's operated over the Atlantic, probably in search of convoys, to the west of the Bay of Biscay, but no attacks were reported.

The main GAF fighter activity was concentrated against landing operations; little opposition was encountered by Eighth Air Force heavy bombers. *There was no immediate fighter reaction on 6 June, when provisional estimates amounted to only about 70 sorties against the Allied beachheads.* However, the tempo increased on 7 June with the arrival of sizable SEF reinforcements, and the estimated scale of effort rose to about 300 sorties, of which 60/70 were ground attacks. Estimated sorties on 8 June amounted to 525/550 in the battle area, including 75/100 ground attacks, and on 9 June, despite adverse weather conditions for most of the day, the GAF delivered some 500 sorties, including 110/120 ground attacks. These fell off on 10 June, with 60/70 ground attacks out of a total of 260/270 sorties.

There are strong indications that after four days of fairly intensive single-engine fighter operations and Allied night and day bombing of bases, enemy strength was considerably reduced and serviceability was probably not higher than 50 percent. In any event, it is ridiculous to think that the reaction encountered was anything like the force that could have been employed had the GAF high command elected to make a finish fight of it.

Some day the Luftwaffe's historians may publish their side of the story, may tell us why the opposition to the Normandy invasion was so weak. That account will be eminently worth reading.

U. S. GOVERNMENT PRINTING OFFICE: 1945